TOWEL 101 FOLDING

Discover the Wonderful World of Towel Origami

Deanna Campbell

BARNES & NOBLE

N E W   Y O R K

ISBN 10: 0-7607-7959-7
ISBN 13: 978-0-7607-7959-0

3 5 7 9 10 8 6 4

This book was conceived, designed, and produced by
BRIDGEWATER BOOKS
The Old Candlemakers
Lewes, East Sussex BN7 2NZ

Creative Director: PETER BRIDGEWATER
Publisher: JASON HOOK
Editorial Director: CAROLINE EARLE
Art Director: SARAH HOWERD
Project Editor: MANDY GREENFIELD
Designer: JANE LANAWAY
Photographer: CALVEY TAYLOR-HAW
Repro Artwork: RICHARD PETERS, LES HUNT

Printed and bound in Thailand

Contents

Introduction

As the title suggests, this book is dedicated to creating folded models using just the towels from your bathroom—in this case, your own private collection of unique and adorable animals. This technique is a lot of fun and is actually much easier to accomplish than it may appear at first glance.

Cute and cuddly— who could resist?

The origins of towel origami are vague—there is a hint that this art may have begun in ancient Egypt, although the true beginnings more probably lie in the 20th century. Folded towel models of this kind have frequently been appreciated by guests staying on cruise liners and in expensive hotels. So why not bring a little luxury into your own home? After all, it costs next to nothing and is extremely quick and easy to do.

Towel folding requires no special skills or equipment, other than a pile of fluffy towels (and perhaps a few buttons and an accessory or two), a little patience, and the ability to follow a few simple steps per project. Yes, in just six to eight steps you can create any one of 16 delightful animal models to adorn the foot of a bed, the floor, or the shelf in your bathroom, for the pleasure and amusement of your family and house guests—and yourself. Indeed, if you consider washday a boring chore and folding bath towels into neat squares leaves you cold, this could be the book that adds a little sparkle to an otherwise dull task.

Every guest will
squeak with pleasure!

A sitting **rabbit**, an appealing
mouse, and a colorful **snail**
are just some of the towel
projects you can create at home.

Come out of your
shell and impress!

The 16 projects in this book range from a simple, quick-to-make **penguin** and an appealing **turtle** to a medium-size cuddly **panda** and an enormous green **crocodile!** Each project includes easy-to-follow photographs, together with a few helpful tips on how you can vary the models, plus a skill rating telling you its degree of difficulty *(see the box on page 9).*

Each animal takes only minutes to complete, and can be accessorized with button eyes in just a few minutes more (or you can leave the models simply as towel shapes, without any accessories). Never again will your house guests be greeted with a pile of neatly folded towel squares balanced on the end of the bed: Who knows what they'll find next: a **scorpion,** a **snake,** a **donkey** with its own saddlecloth, or even a **whale,** complete with frothy water spout.

From now on, you, your family, and anyone who has the pleasure of visiting your home are guaranteed to have far more fun at bathtime than ever before.

Towel Basics and Tips

All 16 models contained in this towel menagerie are created using a few simple techniques, which are illustrated step-by-step on the following pages. While the basic folding techniques are inspired by traditional paper origami methods, the results—as you can see—are rather different! Accurate folding and the crisp, neat edges that are typical of traditional paper origami have here given way to a softer approach, which includes molding, rolling, and stretching techniques.

THE BASICS

The animal models are all made from ordinary bathroom towels, and no special equipment is required. The models do, however, work a little better if the towels have been freshly laundered (or even starched), because the fabric is slightly stiffer and holds its shape more effectively. Remember to avoid using fabric softeners in your wash cycle—they make the towels softer to the touch, but render them less absorbent.

> Remember, practice makes purrrfect!

Approximate towel sizes

The towels we've used for our models conform roughly to the following sizes, but don't be deterred if your towels are a bit different in size—it doesn't matter too much.

Facecloth:
13 x 13 inches (33 x 33 cm)

Guest towel:
16 x 28 inches (40 x 70 cm)

Hand towel:
20 x 40 inches (50 x 100 cm)

Bath towel:
27 x 51 inches (68 x 130 cm)

Beach towel:
35 x 65 inches (90 x 165 cm)

TOWEL TACTICS

Each animal project includes illustrated steps, which usually begin with a towel laid out flat on a surface such as the floor or a bed. Always follow each step carefully and start with the towel laid out as directed—that is, horizontally or vertically *(see overleaf)*. The orientation of the towel dictates the shape that results.

FINISHING TOUCHES

All the projects suggest optional finishing touches that you can add to your models. However, if you wish you can simply add some spectacles or other accessories of your own that you already have; alternatively, you can leave the animals unadorned. In all cases your towels can quickly be returned to practical use.

OPTIONAL FIXING KIT

Before you embark on your towel-folding tasks, gather together a fixing kit of useful equipment, which might include the following:

SAFETY PINS: used to secure folds and overlaps; they can be safely unpinned when it's bathtime and the model has to be dismantled.

BUTTONS: may be used as eyes for your animal models; a selection of buttons in different sizes is useful, but you can easily leave the projects in this book without eyes, if you wish; or you can make eyes from circles cut out of colored paper.

DOUBLE-SIDED STICKY TAPE: an invaluable aid when it comes to adding features such as eyes and other decorative elements to your animal models.

SCISSORS: an all-purpose pair of scissors is useful for cutting paper to make optional extras.

Skill ratings

Each project is given a skill rating of 1, 2, or 3, which describes its degree of difficulty, as shown below:

SKILL RATING 1

An easy project for novices.

SKILL RATING 2

An intermediate project.

SKILL RATING 3

A more advanced project.

TOWEL TIP

Try to make your model "in situ," or at least somewhere close by. Some of the animal models do not travel well and might collapse if they are lifted and moved too far after completion.

Folds and Techniques

FOLDING IN HALF

This is the first step in many projects, and can be done widthwise or lengthwise to form different shapes, depending on whether the towel is initially laid out horizontally or vertically *(see below)*. The way the towel is folded also affects the position of the hems and towel edges—a factor in the finished appearance.

TOWEL LAID OUT HORIZONTALLY

To fold in half widthwise: bring the left-hand short edge over to meet the right-hand short edge (or vice versa), then use the palm of your hand to flatten out the resulting fold.

To fold in half widthwise with the hem at the center: bring both short edges to meet at the center, then use the palm of your hand to flatten out the resulting folds at each side.

To fold in half lengthwise: bring the lower long edge upward to meet the upper long edge (or vice versa), then use the palm of your hand to flatten out the resulting fold.

To fold in half lengthwise with hem at the center: bring both long edges to meet at the center, then use the palm of your hand to flatten out the folds at each side.

TOWEL LAID OUT VERTICALLY

To fold in half widthwise: bring the left-hand long edge over to meet the right-hand long edge (or vice versa), then use the palm of your hand to flatten out the resulting fold.

To fold in half widthwise with the hem at the center: bring both long edges to meet at the center, then use the palm of your hand to flatten out the resulting folds at each side.

To fold in half lengthwise: bring the upper short edge down to meet the lower edge (or vice versa), then use the palm of your hand to flatten out the resulting fold.

To fold in half lengthwise with hem at the center: bring both short edges to meet at the center, then use the palm of your hand to flatten out the folds at top and bottom.

FOLDING INTO THIRDS AND QUARTERS

These techniques require either two or three equally spaced fold lines to be indicated on the towel, either horizontally or vertically. First make a crease *(see below)*, then simply fold the towel as required, using the crease as guide.

CREASING

Run the tip of your finger firmly across the towel, making a visible crease in its fluffy pile, then use this as a guide for subsequent folds.

FOLDING INTO THIRDS

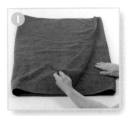

To divide into three horizontally: use the tip of your finger to make two equally spaced creases across the towel, then fold along these creases. Now use the palm of your hand to press the folds flat.

To divide into three vertically: use the tip of your finger to make two equally spaced creases down the towel, then fold along these creases. Now use the palm of your hand to press the resulting folds flat.

Folding into quarters

This follows a similar procedure to folding into thirds:

1 To divide into four horizontally: make three equally spaced creases across the towel. Bring the short sides to meet at the center, then bring the resulting folds together at one side. Now press the shape flat.

2 To divide into four vertically: make three equally spaced creases down the towel. Bring the long sides to meet at the center, then bring the resulting folds together at one side. Now press the folded shape flat.

ROLLING

Rolling is a method that is not used in traditional paper origami. However, the rolling method is very useful when you are creating animal limbs and softly rounded or curved shapes in towels.

THE PARALLEL ROLL

Crease the towel using your fingertip as described above, to indicate the center line. Now roll up one short side toward the marked center line.

Roll up the other half of the towel in exactly the same way toward the center line. The result should be two even rolls that are lying parallel to each other.

THE DIAGONAL ROLL

Begin at a lower corner of the towel, and roll it in a diagonal fashion toward the other side. The result will be a long, thin roll that is tapered at both ends.

Basic Body and Head Shapes

BASIC BODY AND HEAD SHAPES

Most animals have a body of some sort! The menagerie in this book can be created using just a few basic methods—with some variations on the theme to introduce a little versatility. Be sure to read the project instructions carefully, to notice any subtle alterations to the basic form that there may be.

BODY SHAPE 1

This uses the basic rolling technique *(see page 11)* and forms a sturdy shape that stands up extremely well unaided. Some models use this technique with a towel at the center to produce a fatter body shape.

Begin with the basic parallel roll. This can be adjusted slightly if you wish, by making a fold along each long side before rolling, to give a slightly fatter finished shape.

Now grasp the two parallel rolls and bend them gently in the middle. You will see four legs and a body emerging. Arrange the shape so that it stands steadily unaided.

BODY SHAPE 2

This is a bit tricky to perform the first time, but after a few attempts it should take just a matter of seconds. The technique produces a four-limbed form that is more fluid and malleable than body shape 1. It does not stand up unaided, but can be manipulated to sit, lean, or lie down.

Begin with the basic parallel roll *(see page 11)*. Now fold the towel in half, with the rolls facing outward.

Pull out the corner of the towel from the center of each roll. Hold two corners from opposite rolls (a + b) in one hand and two (c + d) in the other hand.

Pull the corners away from each other. The folded towel will stretch out to form two legs and two arms. You can now manipulate the shape as desired.

HEAD SHAPE 1

This diagonal roll *(see page 11)* produces a gently curving triangular form that is extremely useful for making animal necks and heads. The two corners that protrude opposite the rolled point are useful for the creation of ears.

Combination techniques

Some of the projects (for example, the crab and scorpion) require a combination of techniques—say, folding and rolling. Follow the project instructions carefully to achieve the correct result. If in doubt, simply start again!

Begin with a towel placed horizontally, with the center line marked with a crease, as shown. Bring the bottom two corners up to meet the center line, then press the folds flat using the palm of your hand.

Roll up the towel along one diagonal edge toward the center. Do the same with the other side to form an arrow shape.

You will see that as the rolls tighten, the shape begins to curl.

This technique can be customized to form other shapes, with the addition of extra folds—see the individual project instructions for specific details. Here the towel was folded in half widthwise first, to make a shorter shape that is useful for heads.

The Projects

Penguin

These guys always look just like a row of gentlemen in evening dress, queuing up in an extremely orderly fashion. Because this penguin project is made from facecloths, it forms a small, neat shape. Enchant your house guests with two cute penguins arranged on the side of the bathtub, ready to dive into the water.

MAKE YOUR OWN ORIGAMI PENGUIN SKILL RATING 1

Penguins simply have to be black and white—any other combination would not be as effective. Use two square facecloths to make each cute little fellow. Remember, both facecloths must be the same size to give a balanced shape. Check their dimensions before you begin modeling to ensure they are square, and not rectangular.

YOU WILL NEED

- 1 black facecloth
- 1 white facecloth
- 2 small buttons for eyes *(optional)*
- fixing kit *(see page 9)*

Place the black facecloth down flat, then position the white facecloth on top of it, arranging the top so that it lies about 3/4 inch (2 cm) from the top point of the black facecloth underneath.

Take the left-hand and right-hand corners of the white cloth in turn, and fold them underneath to form an arrow shape.

Now tuck the bottom point of the white arrow shape underneath, so that the facecloth resembles a tall triangle in shape.

You can now bring the edges of the black facecloth over the sides of the white triangle toward the center, one quarter of the way across on both sides, as shown.

Place one hand underneath the shape and flip it over to the other side, so that the black side is facing you. Now bring the left-hand edge to meet the right, thus folding the shape in half. Press the shape flat with the palm of your hand.

Pick up the lower front edge of the shape, then bring the lower point of the black facecloth up through the center to form the penguin's tail.

Pinch the folds at the back of the penguin's neck about 2 inches (5 cm) down from the top point, then fold the point over and arrange it to form a beak shape. Press the resulting shape between your fingers to hold the fold secure. Stand the penguin shape upright and open out the base slightly, so that it stands up properly.

TOWEL TIP

Try stuffing the little penguin's body with a couple of tissues, a small bar of soap, or an envelope of bath gel, so that he stands up by himself and has a nice plump tummy.

FINISHING TOUCHES
Gently pull out the black facecloth along the penguin's spine so that it forms a softly curved shape. Use double-sided tape to stick on temporary button eyes.

Cat

• • • • • • • • • •

Prrrr! The sleepy pussy cat in this project would look very comfortable dozing happily at the edge of the bathtub or on a bathroom shelf. Cats are in general averse to water, but perhaps this one is the exception to the rule. Why not place a few colorful bath fizzers next to the towel shape on the tubside so that Kitty has something to play with when she wakes up?

MAKE YOUR OWN ORIGAMI CAT SKILL RATING 3

Tiddles looks great as a tabby, using these patterned towels, but would look equally good in a plain color. Subtle or bold, striped towels can also work very well for this shape. Tiddles could even be a tiger instead, if you choose the right color combinations.

YOU WILL NEED

- 1 beige patterned beach towel
- 2 beige patterned hand towels
- strips of white paper for the whiskers *(optional)*
- 1 medium button for the nose *(optional)*
- sunglasses *(optional)*
- fixing kit *(see page 9)*

TOWEL TIP

You can pad out the body shape using a few facecloths, or even some bars of soap or other toiletries, to make your pussy cat look nice and chubby.

Take the beach towel and roll both short edges to the center. Bend the rolled shape in half, then locate and pull out the four corners of the towel that lie inside the rolls. Pull out two opposite corners (a + b, c + d) at the same time, modeling the towel into the basic body shape 2, following the instructions on page 12.

The resulting body shape has four "legs." Pull corners a and d together to form the front legs, and corners b and c together to form the back legs. Tuck one back leg under the body, and splay the other out to balance the shape. Arrange the two front legs so that the paws curl inward in a catlike manner.

When you are happy with the basic body shape, take a hand towel and roll it up lengthwise into a long, thin sausage. Tuck one end under the body to give it a little height, then curl the roll into a pleasing shape around the body to form the tail.

For the head, you first need to lay the remaining hand towel out horizontally. Fold both short sides to the center and press the folds flat. Now bring the folds to the center and press flat again to form a long rectangular shape.

Roll up the rectangle tightly, beginning at the lower short edge. You can use a couple of safety pins at this stage to ensure the shape does not unroll. Simply secure the edge of the towel at each side to the roll underneath.

Turn the shape around now, so that the towel edge is facing you, and hold it firmly in one hand. With the other hand, grasp the edge of the towel and peel it back on itself, so that it wraps around the rolled shape. This will form the cat's face.

As you pull the edge around the rolled shape, you will see two towel corners protruding from the top. Take these corners and arrange them into two neat triangular points, to form the cat's ears. Secure the head to the cat's body using safety pins.

FINISHING TOUCHES

Cut out strips of white paper for the whiskers and stick them on with double-sided tape, if you wish. You can also add a button nose and a pair of sunglasses as optional extras.

Scorpion

he scorpion is a fiery-looking character, though fortunately the bright red origami scorpion doesn't have a nasty sting in his tail! For added impact, why not make two identical towel scorpions, so that they can dance together in your guest's bed.

MAKE YOUR OWN ORIGAMI SCORPION SKILL RATING 1

This shape is less complicated than it looks—the secret is all in the detail. Make sure that you angle the scorpion's tail very carefully, for a realistic look on the finished origami model.

YOU WILL NEED

2 red beach towels

2 small buttons for eyes *(optional)*

fixing kit *(see page 9)*

Lay one beach towel out horizontally, then place the other towel on top of it, matching up all four edges. Fold the top corners to meet in the center, as shown, and press the diagonal folds flat with the palm of your hand.

Using both hands, roll the right-hand-side diagonal fold toward the center *(see basic head shape 1 on page 13)*. Place one hand near the top of the triangle, then use the other hand to roll up the towel at the other end.

Roll the other diagonal edge in the same way, to form a sharply pointed shape. Now secure the folds together with a safety pin. Slip your hand underneath the shape, then flip it over to the other side, taking care not to loosen the rolls as you do so.

Grasp the edge of the towel that is lying horizontally across the two rolled points at the lower end of the shape. Roll this edge back on itself to open up the shape and form the beginnings of the head and pincers.

Continue to roll this edge up to form the head shape. This will cause the two rolled points to splay out at each side. You can pad out the folds of the head using some bars of soap at this point, if you wish.

When you are satisfied with the head shape, begin to arrange the rolled points to resemble two pincers. Open out the corners of the towel to achieve a good shape.

TOWEL TIP

If your towels are quite soft, you may find that the arched tail will droop a little, so why not insert some crisp tissue paper into the center of the towel before you make the first rolled shape. The paper will then hold the shape more stiffly.

Now that the head and pincers are formed, you can begin to shape the arched body and tail. Hold the body steady while bending the pointed tail in a curve toward the head. You could hide a small bottle of shampoo or bath foam discreetly in the towel folds behind the base of the tail as a support.

FINISHING TOUCHES
Stick on a pair of temporary button eyes using double-sided tape to complete the model.

Crab

· · · · · · · · · · · ·

A bright orange crab would look very comfortable sitting on the edge of the bathtub, ready to jump into the water for a swim. Accessorize your seaside scene with some real shells, starfish, pebbles, and even some shell-shaped soaps.

MAKE YOUR OWN ORIGAMI CRAB SKILL RATING 1

You'll need just one large towel to make this fellow, though the shape translates quite well using smaller sizes, too. Maybe you'd like to make a whole crab family using hand towels.

YOU WILL NEED

1 orange beach towel

2 small buttons for eyes *(optional)*

fixing kit *(see page 9)*

Lay the beach towel out vertically, then fold both long side edges to the center. Now press the folds at both sides flat using the palm of your hand.

Repeat the first step, bringing the sides to meet at the center of the towel. Then press all the folds flat in order to reduce the bulk of the folded shape.

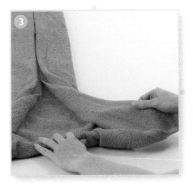

Now open out the lower edge to form the head and claws, taking care not to disturb the folds that run from approximately the center of the towel to the top edge. Roll the center of the lower edge upward, causing the two outer edges to splay out.

Continue to roll up the towel at the center to form a fat, rounded shape that will represent the crab's head. As you do so, the two lower corners will begin to turn inward. Model the two corners to resemble claws.

TOWEL TIP

To make the crab look more realistic, slip a rolled-up facecloth under the finished form to give it a little height.

TOWEL TIP

You can place some scented soaps and a selection of bath time goodies on the back of the crab at step 6, before the shell is completed. Your guests will then have a nice surprise when they open up the towel at bath time.

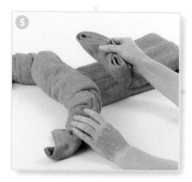

When the head and claws are complete, run your hand along the remaining folds to flatten them out again. Bring the top edge downward and tuck it behind the head shape formed in the previous step.

Flatten out the folds, using the palm of your hand, then bring the new top fold downward to lie on top of the crab's head. This double fold will, with a little manipulation, form the crab shell.

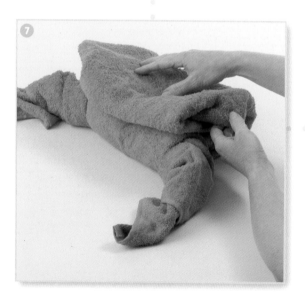

Place one hand on top of the folded shape, just to keep it in place, then put your other hand inside. Pull out the fold from inside to make an oval-shaped shell, then do the same on the other side to create a symmetrical form.

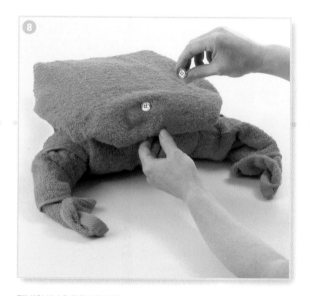

FINISHING TOUCHES

As an optional extra, you can stick on button eyes using double-sided sticky tape.

Mouse

· · · · · · · · · · · · · · · · · ·

"Eeek ... a mouse!" Not to worry—even the most mouse-phobic house guest will be enchanted by this cute little towel animal, complete with beady eyes. Just for fun, you might want to make a cat *(see pages 20–23)* to keep him company.

MAKE YOUR OWN ORIGAMI MOUSE SKILL RATING 3

Fluffy pink towels were used to make this little mouse, but the design also works very well with white, gray, or other pastel shades. And instead of using pink cord for the tail, as suggested, you could simply braid a few strands of pink knitting wool together to serve the same purpose.

Fashion the beach towel into basic body shape 2, following the instructions on page 12. This method can be a bit tricky to perform, so you may need a few attempts to get it right. The result will be a small torso with four legs.

YOU WILL NEED

1 pink beach towel

1 pink hand towel

3 small buttons for eyes and nose *(optional)*

piece of pink cord for the tail *(optional)*

fixing kit *(see page 9)*

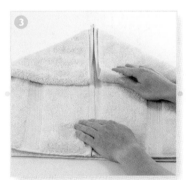

Lay the shape down, with two legs pointing forward and the other two pointing backward. Tuck the two back legs under the body and rearrange the folds to make a pleasing shape. You can pad out the central body folds with bars of soap or a facecloth to give a little more volume around the tummy area, if you wish.

For the mouse's head, take the hand towel and lay it out horizontally. Bring both side edges to meet at the center, then press the folds flat with your palm. Now bring the top two corners down to meet at the center, forming a pointed shape.

Flatten the diagonal folds made in the previous step using the palm of your hand, then bring the lower edge up to meet the point at the top. The top two corners will eventually form the mouse's ears.

You can now begin to form the head. Roll up both lower corners tightly to meet at the center point. This will form quite a bulky, pointed shape.

You will see that the two rolls meet at the center front of the head, and to keep them securely in place you will need to use a safety pin. Simply pin the rolls together at the top, making sure the pin is hidden in the towel's pile and cannot be seen.

When the head is secured, manipulate the top two loose corners to form rounded ears, as shown. You can use gray felt or card inside the ears as ear linings to accentuate the shape, if you wish. Now secure the head to the mouse's body with safety pins.

FINISHING TOUCHES
Stick on temporary button eyes and nose with double-sided tape, if you wish, and add the piece of pink cord for a tail.

Snake

. . . .

A simple but extremely effective toweling snake can be created in just a few minutes using two beach towels. If you use patterned towels, like the ones shown here, they help to convey the markings on the snake's body. It's small details like this that make a difference to the finished model.

MAKE YOUR OWN ORIGAMI SNAKE SKILL RATING 1

The main snake body is simply a long towel sausage coiled into shape. The graceful arched head is formed by rolling the remaining towel diagonally, which allows the fabric to stretch and bend more easily. Add a pointed ribbon tongue, if you wish, and your snake is ready for action.

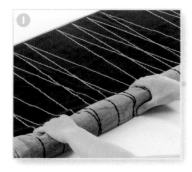

Lay one of the beach towels out horizontally, then roll it up into a sausage shape, beginning at the lower edge. This will form the snake's body.

YOU WILL NEED

2 gray patterned beach towels

2 medium buttons for eyes *(optional)*

piece of red ribbon for the tongue *(optional)*

fixing kit *(see page 9)*

Wind the sausage into a loose coil, in a clockwise direction, then place the coiled towel on a flat surface ready for the next step. Secure the overlap using a large safety pin at this stage, to prevent the coil from unrolling.

Lay the second beach towel out horizontally, as before. Now pick up the left-hand edge and fold about 10 inches (25 cm) of the towel toward the center. Press the fold flat using the palm of your hand. The double thickness of this extra fold gives the head part greater stability.

Remove the safety pin from the body coil to release the overlap. Now tuck the rolled end of the body into the pointed end of the diagonal head and neck roll, then secure once more using the same safety pin. Wrap the head and neck roll around the body coil.

Now pick up the bottom right-hand corner and roll it diagonally toward the other corner *(see the diagonal roll on page 11)*, to form a long sausage shape that is pointed at one end and a little squarer at the other.

TOWEL TIP

This hissing sssssnake would look fabulous sitting in a shallow basket—or perhaps you could find a place for him on top of the laundry basket.

When you are satisfied with the head shape, begin to arrange the rolled points to resemble two jaws. Open out the corners of the towel to achieve a good shape.

FINISHING TOUCHES

As optional decorations for the snake, stick on button eyes with double-sided tape. Cut a V in one end of a piece of red ribbon and stick the other end in the snake's mouth, to make a forked tongue.

Snail

• • • • • • • • • • • • • • • • •

Keen gardeners wouldn't consider a giant snail a welcome sight in the great outdoors—a few hungry, normal-size snails can do a lot of damage to precious plants. However, the bathroom is a very different environment, and the towel snail that follows doesn't present much of a threat at all.

MAKE YOUR OWN ORIGAMI SNAIL SKILL RATING 1

The snail shape follows similar principles to the snake *(see pages 36–39)*, with just a few variations here and there to ring the changes. Use a few large safety pins to make sure the head and neck stay upright, then simply pin the neck securely to the shell coil when the model is complete.

TOWEL TIP

If you do not have a second beach towel, use two smaller bath towels rolled up together to make a nice fat snail shell.

For the shell, lay the striped beach towel out vertically. Bring both side edges to meet at the center, then bring the side folds to meet at the center, too. Now fold the towel in half lengthwise.

1 Lay the yellow beach towel out horizontally, then make a crease vertically down the center of it using your fingertip. Bring both bottom corners up to meet the center crease line, to form a wide, pointed shape. Press the folds flat using the palm of your hand.

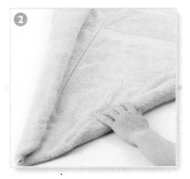

2 Roll each diagonal fold in turn toward the center *(see basic head shape 1 on page 13)*, to form a narrow, pointed shape. This will become the snail's body and head, with a bit more manipulation. Now flip the shape over to the other side and secure the rolls with a safety pin.

Roll up the folded band loosely from one end. Do not squash the folds flat as you do so, for it is better if the shell is quite fat and rounded in shape. Secure the overlap with a large safety pin.

Take the body shape and place it so that the pointed head end lies to your left; the two rolled ends will form the tail. Place the coiled shell onto the body, as shown.

Bend the neck backward toward the shell and make a sharp curve near the top to form the head. This curved shape may need securing with a few pins to ensure that it stays put when the model is complete.

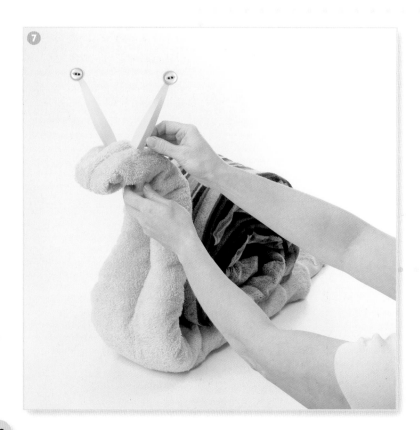

TOWEL TIP

A striped beach towel was used to make the coiled shell on this snake, but you could equally use a plain-colored towel in a contrasting color to the body, such as green. Alternatively, you could pick up accent colors in your bathroom.

FINISHING TOUCHES

To finish the model, cut out tapered rectangles of yellow paper with circles at one end for the horns, then fold them in half and stick them to the snail's head with double-sided tape. Add small buttons as eyes to the circles at the top of the horns.

Rabbit

· · · · · · · · · · · · · · · · · ·

Children will be unable to resist a fluffy bunny, so any parent who is experiencing battles at bath time could try using this model to encourage reluctant, grubby small people into the tub. Hide a few goodies in his tummy for the children to find, as an added incentive.

MAKE YOUR OWN ORIGAMI RABBIT SKILL RATING 2

Rabbit will stand very steadily by himself, but make sure the safety pins secure the beach towel quite tightly around the central rolled towel—otherwise it will be too floppy to support the head. Alternatively, you could use two toilet paper rolls as the central body support, instead of the white bath towel.

YOU WILL NEED

- 1 white bath towel
- 1 blue beach towel
- 1 blue hand towel
- 2 medium buttons for eyes and 1 small button for the nose *(optional)*
- 1 white facecloth for the tail
- fixing kit *(see page 9)*

TOWEL TIP

You could substitute the white facecloth for the tail with a white body buffer, or even with a large round bath fizzer.

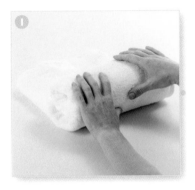

Take the white bath towel and lay it out vertically. Fold it in half by bringing the left-hand edge to meet the right-hand edge, then press the fold flat. Fold it in half again in the same way, then roll up the shape tightly, beginning at the lower edge. This forms a neat cylindrical support for the bunny's body.

Lay the blue beach towel out horizontally and fold it in half widthwise, then fold the upper and lower edges to the center. Now place the roll formed in step 1 in the center, and wrap the upper and lower edges of the larger towel around it, as shown.

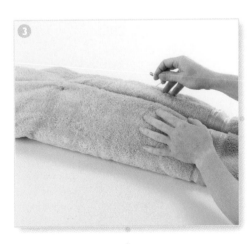

Secure the overlapped edge to the roll underneath using two large safety pins, as shown. This will hold the larger towel in place in readiness for the next step. The bunny's arms and legs will require firm manipulation.

In order to form the hind legs, first flip the shape over so that it is resting on the overlap. Now roll up the edge of the towel, and as you do so the overlapped corners will begin to splay out.

Stand this end on a flat surface, making sure that the overlap edge is in the front. Manipulate the rolled hind legs so that the bunny will stand up steadily by himself, then roll down the top edge to form the front legs in the same way.

Lay the hand towel out horizontally and make a crease at the center with your finger. Fold the bottom two corners up to meet at the center, then fold the lower point up to meet the upper edge. Roll up the towel along both diagonal edges.

Flip the shape over and arrange the top free corners to form two floppy ears, then secure them using a safety pin. Secure the head to the rabbit's body.

FINISHING TOUCHES

Stick on temporary button eyes and nose with double-sided tape, and add a white rolled-up facecloth for a tail, to finish the rabbit model.

Whale

· · · · · · · · · · · · · · ·

"Ahoy there!" Ever fancied a bit of whale-watching from the comfort of your own bathroom? You don't even have to set foot aboard ship! It's easy to make your own pod of whales in various sizes using blue bathroom towels, following the step-by-step instructions opposite.

MAKE YOUR OWN ORIGAMI WHALE SKILL RATING 1

Create your very own Moby Dick using two blue beach towels, then add two white facecloths to create the water spout at the top of his head. This model would also work well in gray or even white. Alternatively, to create a stir in the bathroom, use black towels, then wrap a white facecloth around the chin to make a killer whale!

For the whale tail and body support, take one of the beach towels and lay it out horizontally. Fold it roughly into three by bringing the upper and lower edges to the center and overlapping them. Roll the left-hand end up loosely toward the center.

Stand the rolled part on end, then open out the folds at the other end of the towel. Now fashion the hem into a nice pointed whale tail.

For the main body shape, take the remaining beach towel and lay it out vertically. Fold it in half by bringing the top and lower edges to meet at the center. Now fold the shape roughly into three by bringing the side edges toward the center and overlapping them. Do not flatten out any of the folded edges, because they will help to create a fuller finished shape.

Now pick up the folded shape and wrap it around the rolled body support created in step 1. Overlap the edges at the back of the emerging whale shape. The overlap will be hidden behind the finished model.

You can secure the overlapped edges using a few safety pins, if necessary, to keep the towel in place. Mold the towel into a soft shape over the support beneath. In order for the shape to look whalelike, it needs to be quite bulky, but smooth.

Now take the two facecloths and roll each of them diagonally from one corner, to form two neat rolls that are tapered at both ends.

TOWEL TIP

To look authentic, the whale's body needs to be quite a bulky shape. If your whale looks a bit on the skinny side, try padding the body shape with an additional rolled-up guest towel; or perhaps you could hide some spare toilet paper rolls inside.

Tuck one end of both rolls into the opening in the folds at the top of the whale's head and then fashion them into the shape of a frothy water spout.

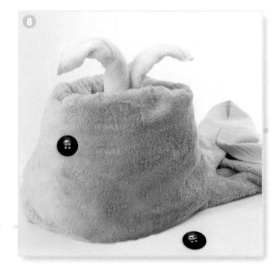

FINISHING TOUCHES
Stick on temporary button eyes with double-sided tape, if you wish.

Crocodile

· ·

"Never smile at a crocodile!" Wow, this guy has what you could call a really toothy grin. However, our toweling model is perfectly harmless and isn't actually likely to eat anyone for lunch.

MAKE YOUR OWN ORIGAMI CROCODILE SKILL RATING 2

"And make it snappy!" This model makes quite a large shape, so ensure that you place your croc on a wide shelf, across the foot of a bed, or on the bathroom floor, so that he has room to stretch out his long tail. A rather bright green was used to make this crocodile, but a darker shade would be equally effective. Or try a towel with a heavy texture, to emulate the crocodile's thick skin.

To make the head, lay the hand towel out horizontally, then fold it into three equal parts by bringing the short side edges inward and overlapping them at the center. Roll the top and lower edges to meet at the center. Secure the rolls together at the center using a large safety pin.

Take one of the beach towels and model it into basic body shape 2, following the instructions on page 12. Lay the shape on a flat surface and arrange the legs as shown. The back legs can be tucked under the body, while the two front legs can be splayed out toward the front.

YOU WILL NEED

2 green beach towels

1 green hand towel

2 large buttons for eyes *(optional)*

fixing kit *(see page 9)*

Slip your hand under the rolled head shape and flip it over to the other side. Now rest it between the front legs of the crocodile, making sure the back edge of the head is butted up against the central body folds.

Take the remaining beach towel and roll it up very loosely in a diagonal fashion, beginning at the lower right-hand corner, to form a long sausage shape that is tapered at each end. This will form the tail, the back, and the eye sockets on top of the crocodile's head.

Fold one pointed end of the towel under the rolled sausage shape, as shown. This will form the basis for the crocodile's eyes and will hide the join between head and body.

Now lay the rolled sausage shape onto the crocodile's body. Fashion one end into a long, slightly wavy shape for the tail, and place the thicker part of the roll along the body.

FINISHING TOUCHES

Stick on temporary button eyes with double-sided tape in the space formed between the towels in step 5.

Hippo

· ·

In the wild, hippos are usually found wallowing happily in lovely, cool mud pools to keep their temperature down during the midday heat. Fortunately, our hippo has never seen a mud bath in his life—so no big, dirty footprints to clean up!

MAKE YOUR OWN ORIGAMI HIPPO SKILL RATING 2

Use your largest and fluffiest beach towels for this model: the emphasis is on the nice plump body shape and wide nose that are characteristic of a real hippo. If necessary, you can use a different-colored towel for the inner layer in step 2, because it will not be seen when the model is complete.

YOU WILL NEED

- 2 gray hand towels
- 2 gray beach towels
- 4 medium buttons for eyes and nostrils *(optional)*
- fixing kit *(see page 9)*

TOWEL TIP

If you do not have any large beach towels, try using two hand towels overlapped at the edges. You can hold the edges together securely with safety pins. The model will not be spoiled if there are a few hems showing here and there.

Lay one hand towel out vertically, and fold it in half by bringing the long side edges together. Repeat once more, but do not flatten out the resulting folds. Now roll up the folded shape loosely, beginning at the right-hand edge, to form a fat cylinder. This creates the bulk of the body shape.

Lay the two beach towels out horizontally, one on top of the other, then place the rolled-up cylinder horizontally in the middle. Bring the top and lower edges to meet the cylinder at the center. Loosely roll up both short edges so that the rolls touch the ends of the central cylinder.

Wrap the top and lower folds of the beach towel around the central cylinder and secure the edges in the middle with a large safety pin, as shown. Now slip your hand under the shape and flip it over to the other side.

You will now see the beginnings of a plump hippo body. Tuck the back legs under the body a little so that the back arches slightly. The two front legs can splay out and point forward.

For the hippo's head, lay out the last hand towel horizontally. Fold the towel into three widthwise, then bring the short side edges to meet at the center, as shown. Flatten out the folds using the palm of your hand.

Roll up the left-hand edge toward the center, then do the same with the other side to make a symmetrical shape. Use a large safety pin to hold the rolls together at one end of the shape. The other end can be left free, in order to form a wider nose shape.

Now flip the rolled head shape over to the other side. Place your hand into the rolls at the top edge and locate two corners of the rolled-up towel. Pull these corners outward gently and then manipulate them to form two cute hippo ears. Lay the head on top of the front legs—you can angle it a little to give the hippo a bit of character.

FINISHING TOUCHES

To complete the model, stick on temporary button eyes and nostrils with double-sided tape.

Donkey

The toweling donkey is easily made from basic body and head shapes, with the addition of a pair of lovely floppy ears. Details such as the saddle and bridle transform a very simple model into a really cute character. Try adding a monogram to the facecloth saddle—you could make one for each of your house guests or members of your family.

MAKE YOUR OWN ORIGAMI DONKEY SKILL RATING 2

This shape is not difficult to make and translates well for other animals: for example, a zebra using black and white striped towels, or a cow or a horse using brown patterned towels. The donkey can also be made to lie down, simply by tucking the rolled legs underneath the central body part.

YOU WILL NEED

2 beige beach towels

piece of beige tasseled cord for the tail

1 beige hand towel

1 beige facecloth

3 yards (2.7 m) of ribbon for the bridle *(optional)*

2 medium buttons for eyes *(optional)*

1 colorful striped facecloth for the saddle

fixing kit *(see page 9)*

TOWEL TIP

Instead of using a length of tasseled cord, you could use a second beige facecloth rolled up diagonally to form the donkey's tail.

Lay one of the beach towels out horizontally, then place the other beach towel on top of it and fold both sets of short side edges to the center. Roll the folded shape from the lower edge to the center, then do the same from the upper edge *(see basic body shape 1 on page 12)*. Try not to make the rolls too tight and do not flatten out any folds, for this would make the shape too skinny.

Grasp the rolls firmly at each end and bend the shape in the middle, as shown, to form the body and the four legs. Stand the donkey body on a flat surface and splay out the folds a little at the base of each leg, to give the shape greater stability. Now secure the tasseled cord tail to the donkey with a safety pin.

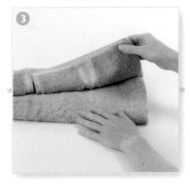

For the head, lay the hand towel out horizontally and bring the short side edges to meet at the center. Fold the shape equally into three, beginning with the lower edge, then press the folds flat using the palm of your hand.

Pick up the lower right-hand corner and roll it diagonally toward the center. Do the same with the other side to form a symmetrical shape. Use a large safety pin to hold the shape secure, then flip it over to the other side.

For the floppy ears, take the facecloth and lay it out flat. Roll it up loosely from one corner, leaving a triangular point free at the center.

Fold the diagonal facecloth roll in half, as shown, then place it on top of the donkey's head. Hold it securely in place with a safety pin. Arrange the ears so that they stand up proudly.

FINISHING TOUCHES

If you wish, use lengths of ribbon to make a bridle, following the picture as a guide. Stick on temporary button eyes using double-sided tape. Secure the donkey's head to the body.

Take the striped facecloth and fold the bottom left- and top right-hand corners to the center. Press the folds flat using the palm of your hand, then flip the shape over to the other side. Place the facecloth onto the donkey's back, like a little saddle.

Turtle

· · · · · · · · · · · · · · · ·

Our toweling turtle is quite at home either in or out of the water. You can rest him on the foot of a bed or balance him on a shelf or laundry basket beside the bathtub. Just for fun, you could use small facecloths to make the turtle's body and head, with a large, oval-shaped bar of soap to represent the shell.

YOU WILL NEED

YOU WILL NEED

1 pale green beach towel

1 dark green beach towel

1 pale green hand towel

2 medium buttons for eyes *(optional)*

fixing kit *(see page 9)*

TOWEL TIP

If you do not have a second beach towel, you could use two smaller bath towels rolled up together to make a nice fat turtle shell.

MAKE YOUR OWN ORIGAMI TURTLE SKILL RATING 3

The turtle is made of three towels and is a bit of a balancing act, so make sure that you construct him "in situ," for he might fall apart if he's moved too far once he's completed. Try twisting the turtle's head gently so that it sits at a slight angle—this gives the model more character.

Take the pale green beach towel and model it into basic body shape 2, following the instructions on page 12. Lay the body shape on a flat surface and arrange the legs as shown.

For the shell, take the dark green beach towel and lay it out horizontally, then fold it in half by bringing both side edges to meet at the center. Now fold the shape into three by bringing the sides toward the center and overlapping them.

To complete the shell, fold the shape into three in the same way as before, but this time bring the lower and upper edges toward the center and then overlap them. Secure the resulting square shape using a safety pin.

Flip the shape over to the other side and place it on top of the turtle's body. Slip your hands into the shape at each side and pull out the folds located on the inside. You can now begin to mold the edges and corners to make a plump, rounded shape.

For the head and neck, take the pale green hand towel and lay it out horizontally. Make a crease in the center with your fingertip, then bring the bottom two corners upward to meet the crease and form a pointed shape.

Fold up about 3 inches (8 cm) at the bottom point, then roll both diagonal edges tightly toward the center *(see basic head shape 1 on page 13)*. This will cause the pointed end to curl up slightly. Secure the rolls together with a safety pin, then flip the shape over.

TOWEL TIP

Use the space under the turtle shell as a handy hiding place for a bath sponge and for lots of bath time treats for your house guests.

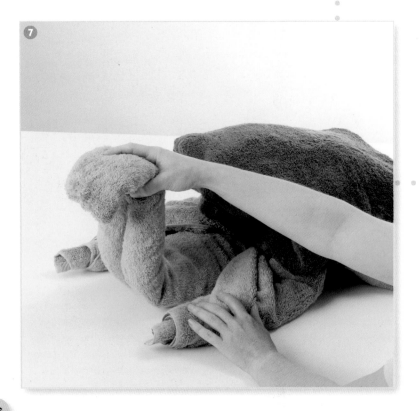

Tuck both the two free ends under the turtle's body, leaving the curved neck and head protruding from the front. Bend the neck a little more to form an arched shape. Curl the end of the neck over to form a head, then secure it with a safety pin.

FINISHING TOUCHES
Stick on temporary button eyes with double-sided tape, if you wish.

Pig

"Oink, oink!" No, you're not seeing things. There could well be a big, fluffy pink pig in your bathroom—not a flying one, however. Pigs are popularly perceived as grubby creatures, but are in fact known to be quite clean animals, so I guess finding one in the bathroom shouldn't be such a surprise.

MAKE YOUR OWN ORIGAMI PIG SKILL RATING 2

Piggy needs to be a nice fat shape, so make sure that you plump out the body well before arranging the head. Add an extra hand towel to the roll in step 1, if you don't have two large beach towels to hand. This model is designed to lie flat; if you prefer a more upright shape, use the method described for the hippo (*see pages 56–59*).

YOU WILL NEED

- 2 pink beach towels
- 1 pink hand towel
- 1 pink facecloth
- 2 medium buttons for eyes (*optional*)
- pink and black paper for the tail and nose (*optional*)
- fixing kit (*see page 9*)

TOWEL TIP

This design would work perfectly in miniature, too—imagine piggy with a few little pink piglets following it along the bathroom shelf. Simply use smaller guest towels in the same color.

Lay one of the beach towels out horizontally. Fold it in half widthwise by bringing the short side edges together, then fold it in half again in the same way. Do not flatten out the folds. Roll it up into a loose cylinder shape, beginning at the lower edge.

Lay the second beach towel out vertically and bring both short edges toward the center. Overlap the edges by about 8 inches (20 cm). Now bring both side edges to meet at the center again.

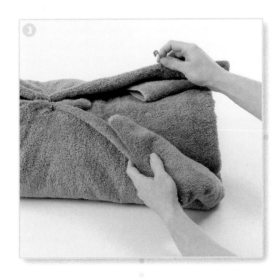

Take the towel roll created in step 1 and place it in the center of the second folded towel. Wrap the upper and lower edges around the roll and secure it with two large safety pins, as shown.

Slip your hand inside the roll and locate the corners that lie inside, just under the secured edges. Pull out all four corners gently, as shown, to create the pig's four legs. Now flip the shape over.

Arrange the legs so that the pig looks comfortable! Then place your hand under its tummy and raise the shape upward a little in the center, so that the back arches slightly. This gives a plumper, more rounded shape.

Now for the piggy's head. Lay the hand towel out horizontally and bring the side edges to the center. Bring the lower edge up to meet the top. Make a 2-inch (5-cm) wide fold along the lower edge.

TOWEL TIP

A spiral of pink paper was used for the pig's tail. However, you could achieve the same effect by twisting a few pink fluffy pipe cleaners together, then winding them around your finger to make a nice curly tail for your bathroom piggy.

Beginning at the lower right-hand corner, roll the towel diagonally toward the center. Do the same on the other side to give a symmetrical shape. Use a large safety pin to ensure that the rolls do not loosen.

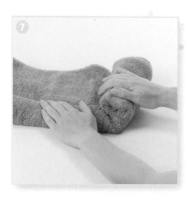

FINISHING TOUCHES

Flip the shape over, then tuck the facecloth in the top to form two floppy ears, and secure the head to the body. Stick on temporary button eyes with double-sided tape. If you wish, cut out a tail and nose from pink and black paper; curl the paper tail using scissors, and stick on the features with small tabs of double-sided sticky tape.

Panda

● ● ● ● ● ● ● ● ● ● ● ●

Y̶ou would be extremely lucky to see a panda in the wild these days, so imagine how
surprised your house guests would be to find their very own panda sitting in the bathroom!
Not exactly the darkest depths of the jungle, but perhaps you can use some bamboo-style

MAKE YOUR OWN ORIGAMI PANDA SKILL RATING 2

This panda is made from a beach towel, three hand towels, and a facecloth, but works well with smaller towels, too. You could make two little panda bear cubs to complete the family, using hand and guest towels. This model has quite a few layers, so remember to use safety pins to hold the shape together.

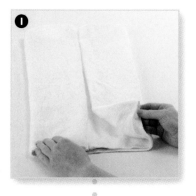

Lay one white hand towel out horizontally. Fold it in half by bringing the sides to meet at the center, then repeat to make a thick rectangular shape. This will form the tummy of your panda.

YOU WILL NEED

- 2 white hand towels
- 1 black beach towel
- 1 black hand towel
- 1 black facecloth
- black and white paper for the eyes *(optional)*
- 1 medium button for the nose *(optional)*
- fixing kit *(see page 9)*

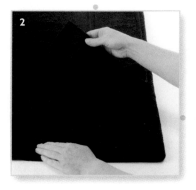

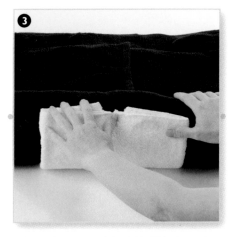

Now take the beach towel and lay it out horizontally on top of the folded white towel. Make sure the white towel lies under the center point of the black one. Using the tip of your finger, divide the black towel into three vertically, then fold the towel along these lines. Now fold the black hand towel in half and place it on top, for extra thickness.

Indicate the center of the folded black towel horizontally, then roll the upper and lower edges to meet at the center point, with the white hand towel on the outside, as shown. The rolled-up sausage shapes will form the panda's legs. Use a safety pin to secure the rolls at the center.

TOWEL TIP

Black and white towels were used to make our lovely panda, but you could use exactly the same methods and white or brown towels to make a polar bear or a grizzly bear for your bathroom.

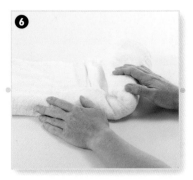

Take the rolled shape in both hands and carefully bend it in half, taking care not to loosen the rolls as you do so. Stand the panda's body on a flat surface and arrange the rolls at each lower leg, so that it is able to stand up firmly by itself.

For the head, take the remaining white hand towel and lay it out horizontally. Fold it in half by bringing the lower edge up to meet the upper edge. Make a 3-inch (7.5-cm) fold along the lower edge, then fold in the side edges to meet at the center.

Take the lower right-hand corner of the folded towel and roll it toward the center of the upper edge. Do the same with the other side to form a triangular shape. Now slip one hand underneath the shape and flip it over to the other side. You can use a safety pin to hold the shape secure at this stage.

Take the black facecloth and fold it in half diagonally, then roll it up loosely from the diagonal edge. Fold the two pointed corners over to form two rounded ear shapes. Now fold the facecloth in half and tuck it into the top of the panda's head. Secure the panda's head to the body with safety pins.

FINISHING TOUCHES

If you wish, cut out eyes from black and white paper and use tiny tabs of double-sided tape on the reverse side to keep them in place on the panda's face. Stick on a temporary button nose as well.

Elephant

· ·

When you visit the zoo, make sure you have a supply of fresh bananas at the ready when it comes to feeding time for the elephants. Hungry elephants are not happy elephants—but our toweling model looks very contented and at ease.

MAKE YOUR OWN ORIGAMI ELEPHANT SKILL RATING 2

You can use plain white towels to make your elephant, but a couple of mid-gray ones give a far more authentic result. Folding your very own Jumbo makes for a stunning display in the bathroom or guest room. Using sunglasses as a finishing touch gives a contemporary look.

YOU WILL NEED

- 1 gray bath towel
- 1 gray hand towel
- sunglasses *(optional)*
- small buttons for eyes *(optional)*

TOWEL TIP

If your bath towel is too big, the elephant's legs may look too long. Simply fold up both short ends a few inches before rolling the towel from the sides to the center. This shortens the legs and makes for a sturdier form.

Lay the bath towel out horizontally, then fold both sets of short side edges to the center. Now find the center of the towel and fold it in half lengthwise. Crease along the fold, then open out the towel again.

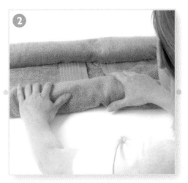

Roll the folded towel from the lower edge to the center, then do the same from the upper edge *(see basic body shape 1 on page 12)*. Don't flatten out the folds or make the rolls too tight, or the shape will end up being too skinny.

Grasp the rolls firmly at each end and bend the shape in the middle, as shown, to form the elephant's body and legs. The body should stand quite steadily by itself, but try opening out the ends of each roll slightly if it seems a bit wobbly.

For the head, lay the hand towel out horizontally and bring the two short side edges to meet at the center. Pick up the lower right-hand corner and roll it diagonally toward the center, as shown *(see basic head shape 1 on page 13)*.

Do the same with the lower left-hand corner, and start to form the trunk. Take care to keep each side of equal thickness. As you continue to roll, the trunk will begin to curl upward.

Flip the shape over to the other side and start to fold the right-hand edge of the towel over the trunk to hold the first rolls in place.

As you continue to roll, two ears will form. Rearrange the folds if necessary so that the head is perfectly symmetrical.

FINISHING TOUCHES

Balance the head on the body or secure it in place with safety pins. Accessorize it with a trendy pair of sunglasses, or use small buttons for temporary eyes.

Index

CREDITS
Towels supplied by Christy
www.christy-towels.com
Stockist no. 08457 585252

PICTURE CREDITS
Jupiter Images Corporation:
    pp.2, 16, 24, 28, 31,
    32, 36, 43, 44, 52,
    55, 56, 59, 60, 64,
    68, 71, 72, 75
Mike Zens/Corbis: p.40
Stuart Westmorland/Corbis:
    p.48